IT'S GOOD...

TO BE GOOD

A DISTINCTLY DIFFERENT BOOK

[AN INSPIRATIONAL POETRY PUBLICATION]

IT'S GOOD...

TO BE GOOD

By
BOSOLA JOSEPH

Published By
DISTINCTLY DIFFERENT
BOOKS AND PUBLICATIONS Ltd
29 Dairy Close, Willesden
London NW10 3RJ

Illustrations in colour
Illustrations © Amaechi Anolue

Set in Tahoma
Printed and Bound in Great Britain by
AXIS EUROPE PLC
Unit 7 Higgs Industrial Estate
Herne Hill Road
London SE24 0AU

A CIP catalogue record for this book is available from the British Library

ISBN 0-9543945-2-6

WITH ALL MY HEARTFELT LOVE

I DEDICATE THIS BOOK TO

MUMMY AND DADDY JOSEPH

CONTENTS

Smile

Understand it will never cost that much to wear a smile

Especially if you insist it's never been your style

But you then fail to realize, it could enrich the day

Of one person who could just pass you by whilst on their way

A smile cannot but radiate your warmth that dwells inside

So truly is there anything that's left than to decide

Encounters with a smile could bring someone else that relief.

So remember it's important you nurture this belief

I'll do the Lot

Whether I'm being watched or not
I'll try my best to do the lot

I'll wake and find the time to pray
Seek God's grace for another day

I'll find the time to make my bed
Not leaving a big mess instead

I'll brush my teeth, try keep them white
Every morning and every night

I'll go to school grasp all I can
Emulate many a great man

I'll do the homework set for me
No matter how hard this may be

I'll strive to do my very best
Giving my loved ones time to rest

Whether I'm being watched or not
I'll try my best to do the lot

What is it all about?

Your life is likened to a day
With a morn, noon and night
The former sees one plan and pray
That all turns out just right

At noon you no doubt hope to see
An accomplishment done
This recognition may not be
Clear-cut for everyone

The evening shoots up and it's time
To sit back and relax
You find many have passed their prime
Cannot retrace their tracks

Nighttime and it is off to bed
Little is left to do
A lot's been done, much has been said
Tired? Most surely too.

Believe your youth is like the morn
Start of your own life's span
Try hard before you're old and worn
To do all that you can.

Value your name

We learn to live and live to learn
What life is all about
Some times it may appear unkind
Confusing? without doubt.

Situations come when you'll hear
The different things folk say
And though a lot may be pleasing
Others could cause affray

Adding to this, it must be said
For no reason at all
Many a person live a lie
A wrong that brings a fall

However one cannot ignore
The good deeds people do
An example of excellence
Worthy to follow too

With this we can't but realise
People are not the same
We live to learn and learn to live
So value your own name.

It's a mistake

A pencil mark can be erased
Should a mistake occur
The chance to make amends, believe
Is what most would prefer

Yet this is not always the case
For people everyday
As opportunities like this
Rarely come by their way

Mistakes are common, take on board
These can cause joy and pain
Understanding one person's loss
Could be another's gain

So if it's thought there's been a wrong
With what you've said or done
Find the time to apologise
It's bound to please someone.

Tick Tock it's the clock

Tick tock it's the clock

With reminders of what's been done
Which with hindsight was seen as fun
Even though it offended one

Tick tock it's the clock

Ready to serve a needy race
With pride, and a longing to place
A warm smile on each persons face

Tick tock it's the clock

Helpful in making each one plan
Despite being ignored by man
Who claim winning a race not ran

Tick tock it's the clock

Prompting that, whatever you do
Time is not bound to wait for you.
This may appear selfish, but true

Tick tock it's the clock

Give it a try

The times which can't be counted
A truth you may deny
Have seen your actions upset one
Without you knowing why.

It could have been a word you said
That did not edify
Or something that you really did
Which did not meet the eye

Maybe you showed no empathy when
You saw a friend cry
Or in the midst of company
You did nothing but sigh

It could have been the way you looked
Eyed that lone passer-by
You may have left a room without
A thank you or goodbye

Accused of something recently
You cannot justify
Rethink in fact correct your ways
Don't fret give it a try

True friends

Perseverance with twin Patience

Indeed have come to stay

Invite them in and then find out

How each can make your day?

Working together, hand in hand

It's rare if found apart

Ardent to do the best they can

Just watch and let each start

Equipped to reach afar and hope

All whom they meet succeed

By no doubt these companions

Are friends that we all need

Make it up

That friend of yours has let you down
In fact it's talk all over town
And you wear nothing but a frown

Crying has proved you less than strong
Startled you wonder what went wrong
A thought that tarries all day long out at play
As one action or word may stray
A likely episode each day

So be a true friend, cast no doubt
On how to bring change, work things out
Consider you have got such clout

Knowing disputes must be resolved
And this means for each one involved
Before a friendship is dissolved.

A word from mum

Mum constantly said why

It did no gain to lie

The sky wasn't that high

And things were worth a try.

She said "in all you do

Hold firm to what is true

Discern what might harm you

Think everything right through"

Insisting, "be sincere

Making intentions clear

Because no matter where

Discredits cost one dear"

Can you?

Can you find a kind word to say?
About a friend at all
If so, pass on a compliment
Make them feel ten feet tall

Can you unearth something they like?
Maybe a favoured song
If so, create that atmosphere
Where they'd love to belong

Can you speak up to encourage one?
Knowing what they've been through
If so, consider this a gift
And use it wisely too

Can you give up, yes spare that time
To help a friend in need
If so believe you've done yourself
A kind and worthy deed

Yesterday, today, tomorrow

Yesterday believe has said goodbye

Played out the part and passed on by

Today accept is right here instead

Learn from the past, and forge ahead

Tomorrow, no doubt is still yet, to come

Just hope it holds a treat for some

Tongue and teeth

Both tongue and teeth work hand in hand
Respecting one another's stand
Attentive to the other's voice
Simply because each has no choice
No matter where placed in the land

Bound by fate, spelling destiny
Ignore each other? This can't be
So when a hiccup causes pain
Resolve must put things right again
Paving the way for harmony

So really what is left say?
Except remind yourself each day
That from the very time you wake
Master and learn to give and take
Whilst watching this move make a way.